D1328267

FAMOUS FAMILIES™

PAUL MCCARTNEY
AND
STELLA MCCARTNEY

TIM UNGS

WITHDRAWN

The Rosen Publishing Group, Inc., New York

Published in 2005 by The Rosen Publishing Group, Inc.
29 East 21st Street, New York, NY 10010

Copyright © 2005 by The Rosen Publishing Group, Inc.

First Edition

All rights reserved. No part of this book may be reproduced in any form without permission in writing from the publisher, except by a reviewer.

Library of Congress Cataloging-in-Publication Data

Ungs, Tim.
Paul McCartney and Stella McCartney / Tim Ungs.
  p. cm.—(Famous families)
Includes bibliographical references.
ISBN 1-4042-0263-3 (library binding)
1. McCartney, Paul—Juvenile literature. 2. McCartney, Stella, 1971– —Juvenile literature. 3. Rock musicians—England—Biography—Juvenile literature. 4. Fashion designers—England—Biography—Juvenile literature.
I. Title. II. Series.
ML3930.M37U54 2004
782.42166'092'241—dc22

                                                                    2004013391

Manufactured in the United States of America

Contents

STELLA TAKES A BOW

For a young fashion designer, the student show is an important milestone. The final requirement for graduation at most design schools, it is a small-scale version of the glamorous catwalk spectacles that are held in New York, Paris, London, and Milan. At the student show, everything an aspiring Yves St. Laurent or Coco Chanel has learned—or hasn't learned—is on display. It is an exciting but extremely stressful time. Students must design and make all the clothes for a collection. To prepare, they must spend long nights sweating the details. They cut cloth, sew, embroider—and worry. Will I get my clothes finished in time? Will people like my clothes? What will people think of me?

It's a tough time for any young designer. Stella McCartney's 1995 debut collection, at London's highly regarded Central Saint Martins College of Art and Design, was no exception. As the daughter of Sir Paul McCartney, one of the world's most famous and

In this photo from the 2000 fashion week in Paris, models strut their stuff dressed in the new collection from the Chanel fashion house. Karl Lagerfeld, then head designer for Chanel, was the man behind these fabulous creations.

Stella's designs are among megastar Madonna's favorites. In this photograph, Stella and Madonna pose for the press backstage after the 1999 VH-1/*Vogue* fashion awards.

beloved musicians, Stella faced advantages and disadvantages none of the other students had to contend with. Of course, she had a little help from her friends. While most student designers settle for inexperienced models to wear their fashions for the show, Stella had supermodels Naomi Campbell and Kate Moss strolling the runways in her fashions. Many students had to struggle to come up with appropriate music. Stella had no such problem there, either. Her father wrote a song called "Stella Mayday" especially for the occasion. Naturally, Sir Paul and Stella's mother, Linda, were sitting front and center to show support for their daughter.

But, as Stella would find out over the course of her career, famous friends and family can be a blessing and a curse. Normally, student fashion shows are low-profile affairs, attracting only the designers themselves, their family members, friends, and teachers. In contrast, at Stella's show, there were reporters and photographers from all over the world. Many of them had prejudged Stella as being a celebrity daughter playing at fashion, as opposed to being a serious designer. All that attention meant the stakes were very high for Stella.

In deciding to go into fashion, Stella had chosen a difficult profession. Few industries are as competitive. But Stella had been given a loving and supportive head start by her parents. Everyone knows about the worldwide fame Stella's father achieved as a member of the Beatles, the most celebrated rock group in history. Fewer are familiar with Paul's (and Linda's) other great achievement, raising a well-adjusted family at a time when rock stars' personal lives were most often associated with drugs, divorce, extravagant demands, and antics such as destroying hotel rooms.

The McCartneys, one of the world's most famous couples, made the remarkable decision to have a normal family. It seemed like a highly unrealistic goal, yet they succeeded in raising grounded, unspoiled, and confident children. Paul and Linda made every effort to shield their children from the public eye. Instead of living in a mansion with maids and nannies—as most rock stars chose to do—the McCartneys lived in a tiny farmhouse in the English countryside that was surrounded by woods. Rather than sending their children to fancy boarding schools, they sent them to local comprehensive schools (the British equivalent of American public schools). Stella shared a bedroom with her sister, Mary, her half-sister, Heather, and her brother, James. The house had one bathroom. The children had farm chores to do. If they wanted money beyond a small allowance, they had to earn it.

All this meant that when Stella decided that she wanted to have a career in the fashion industry, she did not expect it to be handed to her. Instead, she got a series of jobs to gain experience in all aspects of the industry. Without question, her name opened doors. Few young girls would be considered for an internship with a prestigious fashion

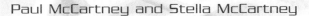

Stella's first show for the Chloé design label was the 1998 autumn/winter collection. Here, Linda and Paul proudly watch their daughter's show, along with the rest of the fashion world.

magazine like British *Vogue* or as an apprentice with French designer Christian Lacroix. However, Stella was always willing to work hard to prove that she deserved the opportunity her name had given her. As Betty Jackson, one of Stella's early employers, told *Vogue*, "The name [McCartney] closes as many doors at it opens. I was very severe when I interviewed her, poor thing, because I didn't really want a pop star's daughter working for me. I thought it would be far too disruptive. Of course, when she came, she couldn't have been any more diligent and less grand, arriving at 9:30 AM sharp every day, making the tea and coffee, always asking the machinists [sewing machine operators] how their weekends were and not saying a thing about her own, despite the fact her weekend bag might have had a Concorde sticker on it."

On the eve of her student show, Stella's hard work paid off in a big way. The clothes she had made expertly blended men's tailoring with a feminine touch. They were elegant, beautifully constructed, and sexy. Other students may have grumbled about the commotion caused by Stella and her celebrity family and friends, but the fact was that Stella's work was simply better and more polished. Her student show got rave reviews. More important, since, above all, fashion is a business, she immediately attracted the interest of a buyer for Tokio, a London boutique. Her career was under way. And what a career it would become. Just two short years after her graduation show, Stella got the job of head designer at Chloé, a highly respected fashion design company in Paris.

One person who has never been surprised by Stella's success is her father. Sir Paul recalls being amazed by his daughter's skills when he once visited her at the Chloé studio. As he told the *New Yorker*, "I've watched her in the atelier [studio], and she'll be saying, 'Um, need a bit more bias [slant, angle] on here, this hem's got to come up a bit—wait a minute, give me this, it's the wrong material, change it.' And they all say, 'Oui, Madame, oui, Madame.' I just stand there and think, This is it—this is the real thing. When she started, people said, 'She's a bit young, it's a big job, she's twenty-five'—and I said, 'Yeah, well, the Beatles made Sgt. Pepper [their most famous album] at twenty-five, and we weren't too young for that.' She's just brilliant. And she's my little baby."

CHAPTER 1

FROM LIVERPOOL TO BUCKINGHAM PALACE

James Paul McCartney was born at the height of the Second World War (1939–1945) in Liverpool, England, on June 18, 1942. Though the years after the war ended in 1945 were difficult, Paul had a happy childhood. His father, James, was a cotton salesman. His mother, Mary, whom he would make famous forever in the song "Let It Be," worked as a midwife until her life was cut short by cancer when Paul was barely in his teens.

Skiffle Days

In spite of the fact that he never learned to read a note (and failed his audition for the Liverpool Cathedral choir), Paul embraced music wholeheartedly. As a teenager, he joined a series of bands that played an early form of rock 'n' roll known as skiffle. One day, after a church concert, Paul ran into another

Here, Paul sings with the Beatles at a 1963 club show in Liverpool, England, his hometown. This small, intimate Beatles show is vastly different from the stadiums of screaming fans for whom they would soon be playing.

skiffle enthusiast named John Lennon. John asked Paul to join his band, the Quarrymen. In 1960, when they were still teenagers, Paul and John changed their band's name to the Silver Beatles and relocated the group to Hamburg, a gritty German port city with a roaring nightlife. They began to develop their sound playing virtually all night long to rowdy crowds in beer cellars. For a couple of years, they traveled back and forth between Hamburg and Liverpool. In doing so, they gathered huge local followings.

The Big Break Arrives

In late 1961, the group—known simply as the Beatles—caught a huge break when they auditioned for two record companies. Decca Records turned them down—a decision that they would later greatly regret. However, another company, Parlophone, signed Paul and John, together with George Harrison (guitar) and Ringo Starr (drums), to a contract. By early 1963, the group was producing hit singles in England, nearly all of which were cowritten by Paul and John. This was unusual. "They made writing your own material expected, rather than exceptional," noted fellow songwriter Elvis Costello in a tribute in *Rolling Stone* magazine. "Every record was a shock when it came out . . . [T]he Beatles sounded like no one else. They had already absorbed [rock 'n' roll pioneers] Buddy Holly, the Everly Brothers and Chuck Berry, but they were also writing their own songs."

The Ed Sullivan Show: The Birth of Beatlemania

On a Sunday evening in February 1964, the Beatles played live on *The Ed Sullivan Show* to what was then the largest TV audience ever. Their

This 1964 photograph shows the Beatles during their legendary appearance on *The Ed Sullivan Show*. Paul, as animated as always, is on the far left. George Harrison plays lead guitar in the middle, and John Lennon, playing rhythm guitar, is on the right. The famously witty Ringo Starr plays drums behind them.

performance was an event people would remember for the rest of their lives. "You could not hear them playing anything," an associate director for *The Ed Sullivan Show* told *Rolling Stone*. "The noise was incredible. Nobody could hear a thing except the kids in the audience, screaming. They overpowered the amplifiers. The cameramen couldn't hear. Even the kids couldn't hear anything, except each other screaming." A production assistant who remembered Elvis Presley's *Ed Sullivan* appearance a few years earlier noted that "the reaction of the

The Beatles in the Guinness Book of World Records

EMI, the Beatles' record company, has estimated that the Beatles have sold more than 1 billion discs and tapes worldwide. A song Paul wrote for the Beatles, "Yesterday," is the most recorded song. There were 1,600 versions of "Yesterday" recorded by other artists between 1965 and 1986. One of their albums, *The Beatles 1*, sold 13.5 million copies around the world in its first month, making it the fastest-selling album of all time.

kids [to Elvis] was nothing close to what it was for the Beatles."

Also in 1964, Capitol Records, an American label, picked up the option to sell the Beatles' records in the United States. The phenomenon known as Beatlemania was in full swing. Everywhere they went, John, Paul, George, and Ringo were met by screaming mobs of teenage girls. For all their appeal to the younger generation, the Beatles also succeeded in convincing parents and the news media that they represented the end of civilization. Love them or hate them, with their trademark shaggy haircuts, they were perhaps the most recognized faces on the planet.

To keep things in perspective, it's necessary to remember that the entire span of the Beatles' superstardom lasted only about six years. In 1970, they disbanded, leaving behind as great a collection of music as any rock band is likely to create. Paul McCartney was not even thirty years old when he embarked on the second act of his remarkable life. Just prior to the Beatles' breakup, Paul had married Linda Eastman. Together, they turned their interests to raising a family and retreated to a small organic farm in East Sussex, south of London.

This 1979 photograph captures the psychedelic look and mood of Paul's post-Beatles band, Wings. Linda, Paul's wife and Stella's mother, was a member of the band as well.

After the Beatles: Life Goes On

After the breakup of the Beatles, Paul formed a group called Wings, which featured Linda playing keyboards. Initially, Linda refused, saying she was not talented enough, but Paul insisted she be in the band so that they could be together even when Wings was touring. With Wings, Paul rediscovered his love for playing in front of a live audience. The last Beatles concert had been in 1966, and Paul was thrilled to

Irvington Public Library
Irvington on Hudson, N.Y.

The Beatles, Songwriting, and Pop Music

Of course, the Beatles were much more than just teenagers' heartthrobs. They took their music very seriously. They started with simple rock and pop songs like "Love Me Do," but their music changed rapidly. While George Harrison contributed many songs that went on to become classics, the Beatles' amazing creativity was largely due to Paul and John's unique songwriting partnership. The songs, always credited to Lennon-McCartney, were written separately. Either John or Paul would write most of a song, and the other would help finish it. Their relationship was very intense. Paul and John were competitive, often argued, and were more than a little jealous of each other. Whatever personal tensions were involved in the creative process, the result was an amazingly rich collection of music. Working with the talented producer George Martin, the Beatles sometimes used unconventional instruments, such as Indian sitars, classical string quartets, and even entire orchestras. With albums like *Rubber Soul* (1965), *Revolver* (1966), and *Sgt. Pepper's Lonely Hearts Club Band* (1967), John, Paul, George, and Ringo changed the very definition of rock 'n' roll. They took pop music and transformed it into something close to high art. They were the best and most popular group in the world.

rediscover the energy a live audience gave him. He even took Wings on an unplanned and unrehearsed tour of British universities. He and the band literally drove all over England in a van, looking for places to play. Unannounced, they would show up at a university's student union [activity center] in the afternoon and arrange to play a gig the very same night. Although some critics found Wings' music a bit of a letdown after the Beatles, the fans loved it. The group had seven number-one albums before they disbanded in 1981.

The eighties saw Paul venturing into

new artistic territory, including film (he wrote and starred in *Give My Regards to Broad Street*), poetry, classical composition, and painting. In 1997, he became Sir Paul McCartney when he was knighted for his contribution to the music industry. "Proud to be British, wonderful day, and it's a long way from a little terrace in Liverpool," he told reporters before receiving the ultimate British honor from Queen Elizabeth II.

Through his spectacularly successful post-Beatles career, Sir Paul has done a remarkable job balancing the public life of a rock star and the private life of a father and family man. He remained married to and in love with Linda until her untimely death from cancer in 1998, and he

The newly knighted Sir Paul McCartney shows off his medal in this 1997 photograph. He was knighted at Buckingham Palace by Queen Elizabeth II.

has been a loving and encouraging father to his children. As he told the *New York Times*, "So we lived very basically [in spite of] all the fame, trying to keep some normality." Paul McCartney is one of the few celebrities who could be equally proud of his achievements in the public arena and in the eyes of his children.

CHAPTER 2

HEY, STELLA

As a young girl, Stella McCartney showed few signs of being a fashion diva in the making. A tomboy and the family comedian, young Stella was more interested in riding her horse and playing in mud than dressing up. In fact, she never even owned a doll. As Stella entered her teens, however, her interest in fashion began to emerge. By the age of thirteen, she was designing and making clothes. Surprisingly, her fashion inspiration did not come from fashion magazines. She once complained that she never read *Vogue* magazine because she couldn't afford it. (Indeed, her parents were known for being cheap with allowances.) Her real source of fashion inspiration came from Paul and, especially, Linda. As she would later say in an interview with the *New Yorker*, "They both had a very natural way of being comfortable with themselves, not taking things too seriously or really caring about what people might think—the whole thing of wearing a Saville Row suit with a . . . T-shirt, which is very much my way of doing things. My mum and dad echoed each other, really, in the way they looked."

From the time she was an infant *(inset)*, Stella often accompanied her parents while they toured with their band, Wings. This 1976 photograph shows Paul and Linda's similarities in their fashion sense. Later, as an adult, Stella would use such images of her parents as inspiration for her own designs.

Stella's Fashion Inspiration: Her Mum

Stella was especially inspired by her mother's mix-and-match approach to fashion, blending high fashion (haute couture) with vintage, or with a workaday pair of jeans. "My mum was just really cool," she explained to the *New Yorker*. "I remember going into her wardrobe [closet] when I was a little girl. She had some old Yves Saint Laurent dresses, because she and my dad had gone to some Paris couture shops [shops that sold high fashion, very expensive designer clothes] when they first met, when they were young, but then right next to them were all the juxtapositions—an old vintage thirties dress, then a pair of platform boots, then a T-shirt, then a pair of . . . jeans. That kind of mixture pretty much became my philosophy."

Making It on Her Own

Stella was determined to make her own way in the fashion world. She did not even tell her parents that she was applying for the design program at Central Saint Martins. She feared that they might use some influence on her getting in. As it turned out, the school's directors claimed not to have known that her parents were *the* McCartneys. Once she entered the design program, Stella did not go about her studies in a halfhearted way. When she felt that her coursework stressed the theory of design at the expense of hands-on experience, she got a job as an assistant to a men's suitmaker on London's famous Saville Row. Very few of her fellow students took such pains to learn the nuts and bolts of fashion design.

After her famous success in her student show, Stella set up her own shop and worked hard at learning how to build a network of sources and suppliers. She made an effort to learn what buyers wanted. Her designs were in such demand that she couldn't make them fast enough. Stella soon found that her business was growing too fast for her and two part-time employees. Soon, however, she had an opportunity to make a great career advance. Mounir Moufarrige, the president of Chloé (a well-established and respected French design house that had recently fallen on lean times), offered her a job.

In 1997, at age twenty-five, Stella was hired by Chloé, a leading fashion house in Paris. She replaced the famous designer Karl Lagerfeld.

"The Breath of Fresh Air That Chloé Needs"

That Moufarrige chose a twenty-five-year-old with no high-level experience was a risky move that invited criticism and second-guessing. The man Stella was to replace as Chloé's head designer, fashion legend Karl Lagerfeld, expressed his displeasure with the choice to the press. "I think they should have taken a big name," he sniffed to *Women's Wear Daily* (WWD). "They did—but in music, not in fashion." Stella was hurt but also flattered by being singled out by Lagerfeld. And she showed the confidence needed to survive in the dog-eat-dog fashion world when she proclaimed to *WWD*, "I don't think the Chloé chiefs would

be stupid enough to ride a whole company on me because of who my father is. I'm the breath of fresh air that Chloé needs."

Taking on the new, high-profile job was a great challenge for Stella. It was made even more challenging because at about the same time, her mother was continuing her battle with breast cancer. However, Linda was able to attend Stella's first major show for Chloé in late 1997. As might be expected, both Linda and Paul loved it. "I thought it was excellent, feminine, and sexy," Paul told *WWD*, and the critics agreed. "One minute McCartney showed delicately embroidered peach gowns with overlapping chiffon petals," wrote a fashion journalist in the *San Francisco Chronicle*. "The next [minute] she showed tough-girl studded black faux leather jackets and skintight pencil skirts with silver zippers up the back seam. Somehow it all worked."

With Stella in charge, Chloé's sales took off. During the next four years, the company's revenue reportedly quadrupled. And the label became a hip, hot item with celebrities like Gwyneth Paltrow, Nicole Kidman, and Madonna. Stella even designed Madonna's wedding dress. Stella's success at Chloé won raves from Anna Wintour, one of the most powerful voices in the fashion industry. Wintour told the *New Yorker*, "We have so few women who are really important in the world of fashion, and it's great to have Stella joining the ranks."

In this photograph, Stella appears at the fashion show at which her 1998 prêt-à-porter (ready-to-wear) collection for Chloé debuted. The romantic touch she gives to all her designs is evident in the pieces the models surrounding her are wearing.

In 2000, Stella won a VH-1/*Vogue* award for her work at Chloé. Paul showed up to support his daughter in a humorous T-shirt that reflected the proud papa's thoughts.

Designer of the Year

In 2000, Stella was named the VH1/*Vogue* Designer of the Year, an award presented jointly by *Vogue*, the fashion bible, and VH1, the cable music channel. Presenting the award was none other than Stella's father, Sir Paul. In an amusing demonstration of good-hearted family bonding, Paul wore a T-shirt with the caption "About flippin' time," a reference to a similar shirt Stella had worn to his Rock and

Roll Hall of Fame induction ceremony the previous year. The show of father-daughter togetherness brought laughs and a standing ovation from the audience.

The following year, Stella made her biggest move yet. She left Chloé to form her own company. She was backed by executives of the Gucci Group, who gave her complete artistic control and financial support. Like her father, Stella had reached the top of her profession before the age of thirty.

CHAPTER 3

ALL TOGETHER NOW

Stella has fond memories of her childhood. "It was all very normal . . . Family life was just family life: school, dinner, telly [television], bed," she told the *New Yorker.* She recalled not really understanding what went into her father's musical success. "I used to say to my dad, 'Come on, Dad, put your song in the charts again,'" she explained to the *Daily Telegraph.* "When I was a kid I thought you just put songs in the charts. I didn't know that you had to have like a hit." Stella had no idea of her father's fame until she accompanied Wings on tour to Brazil and saw him playing in front of close to 200,000 enthusiastic fans.

Keeping the Kids out of the Spotlight

The McCartneys took pains to shield their kids from publicity. Paul and Linda were used to paparazzi—the rude masses of celebrity photographers. They could tune them out. However, the children could not, least of all Stella. "I remember we were on holiday

In this 1972 photograph, Paul and Linda travel with three of their children: Stella, Mary, and James. The McCartneys were an extremely close family, and unlike the families of many celebrities, lived a fairly simple life.

When former Beatle John Lennon was murdered in New York in 1980, millions of people around the world grieved. This photograph shows just one of the hundreds of tributes left in New York's Central Park that day.

in Barbados once," she recalled in an article in the *New Yorker*, "and this photographer was taking pictures on the beach, and I got so annoyed that I ran up to him and threw sand in his lens. We basically had to leave the country the next day, because of what I'd done. My dad didn't really notice things like that, because he'd grown up with it."

As much as the McCartneys wanted a quiet life, they certainly had to take more precautions than the average family. The tragic assassination of John Lennon made it clear that the public's interest in the Beatles could have a dangerous edge. However, for most of the time, the McCartney children did not have to worry about the prying eyes of the press and fans. Their life on the farm was happy. Their tiny farmhouse encouraged family togetherness. "We just liked the idea of the kids being on top of us, watching TV around the fire," Paul told the *New York Times*. The everyday routine for the McCartney children involved riding horses, tending sheep, and working in the family's organic garden. Linda is credited with introducing Paul to vegetarianism and animal rights, two causes that were picked up enthusiastically by Stella, who has always refused to have anything to do with leather or fur, two staples of the fashion industry.

Old-Fashioned Parenting

The common image of a rock star's child is that of a spoiled brat. In contrast, the McCartney children had to face old-fashioned discipline when they misbehaved. Once, when Stella was about to attend a Michael Jackson concert with some friends, she sneaked a puff of a cigarette. As she was about to leave the house, her father confronted her and refused to let her go to the show. "That was just like him," Stella later told the *New Yorker*. "He's . . . very old-school [old-fashioned]. 'If you're not back by twelve o'clock, you'll get grounded'—that type of thing."

And just like the other children from their village, Stella and her siblings attended the local comprehensive school. In the mornings, she caught the bus to school. As she noted in the *Daily Mail*, "I was a bit ashamed if I missed the bus and had to be dropped off in a nice car." Linda packed vegetarian lunches (which were a big hit with the other kids) and she picked the children up after school. "There was nothing ostentatious [showy] about them and Linda used to pick them up every day in a Mini [a tiny economy car]. Paul occasionally picked them up in a bigger car . . . and when he turned up everyone got quite excited," a classmate recalled in an article in the *Daily Mail*.

Stella is grateful for having taken a tougher educational path than many children of celebrities. When it comes to having children of her own, she told the *Observer*, "I'd do it exactly the same. Hopefully I'll

be living in the country if I'm lucky enough to have kids, and they'll go to normal schools and nobody will know about them, unless they decide they want to be known about." At times, she may have wished that she had been sent to a fancy private school, but in the end, she knew her parents' decision was the right one. "It was one of the best things that happened to me," she explained to the *Telegraph*. "When you go to a comprehensive and you come from my background, people don't really love you for it. You get a hard time. And that is so valuable as a kid to know that. Otherwise you would just go through life thinking you are fabulous the whole time. People would have said, 'Oh your dad's great. You are great.' They would have been impressed by all the money and all that stuff. It would have been gross. That is so not the way I was brought up."

The Loss of Linda

Both father and daughter faced a terrible loss when Linda died of cancer in 1998 at the age of fifty-six. Linda was the inspiration for Paul's post-Beatles career and for everything Stella has done. "She [Stella] is completely her mother's daughter," Barbara Daly, a lifelong friend of the family's, once told the *Sunday Telegraph*. "Her gutsiness, her set of principles, she learned all that from Linda. They were incredibly close." To this day, even in interviews, Stella often becomes emotional about her mother.

Paul's loss was every bit as great, if not greater. He was married to Linda for three decades. In all that time, they spent a total of ten nights apart. In a public statement he gave to the press immediately after Linda's death, Paul recalled their last moment together: "I said

In this photograph from the late 1970s, Paul and Linda enjoy a stroll with one of their many horses. The McCartneys were famous for their love of animals and their vegetarian lifestyle. Linda even marketed a line of frozen vegetarian dinners.

to her, 'You're up on your beautiful appaloosa [a horse with a spotted coat] stallion; it's a fine spring day, and we're riding through the woods. The bluebells are all out, and the sky is clear blue.' I had barely got to the end of the sentence when she closed her eyes and gently slipped away."

CHAPTER 4

THE LONG AND WINDING ROAD

While Stella's career had taken a great leap forward with the formation of her own fashion house, it was not easy at first. She had to overcome a rocky start as the head of her own company. The first collection for the Stella McCartney label received negative reviews from the fashion press. Stella's spring 2002 show took place in October 2001 (designers always show their collections a season ahead), and many observers thought her collection was perhaps a little tasteless for the subdued mood of the post–September 2001 terrorist attacks. As tough an outward appearance as she projects (one of her nicknames is "Stella Steel"), Stella was really hurt by the negative comments. "People think I am strong, but I just wanted to crawl away [after that show]," she explained to the *Australian Age*. "I thought, I will live in the country with my horse. I'll get a nine-to-five [job], I don't need this." But she persevered, and with her second and third collections, she began to make believers out of many of her critics.

These photographs show pieces from Stella's ready-to-wear collection for her own label during the 2001 *(left)* and 2002 *(right)* fashion week in Paris. Fashion week is held in various cities across the world, so that designers can show the world their latest creations.

Role Model for Girls

Even young girls find much to admire in Stella. A 2003 study carried out by Girlguiding UK (the Girl Guides are roughly the equivalent of the Girl Scouts in the United States and Canada) showed that "40 per cent of the girls questioned admired Stella and thought her to be the best role model in the public eye."

Stella's third show moved a journalist for the *London Times* to remark, "[The] collection . . . managed to be sexy and elegant, cool and delicately pretty at the same time. She has a knowing quality to her style that probably comes from being close to the demographic group [target audience] that tends to love her clothes, which is a rare thing in fashion these days." The review went on to comment on the "fluidity and ease that derives [comes] from [Stella's] instinctive sense of women's bodies and how women want to dress."

Indeed, it is Stella's understanding of women that is perhaps her strongest asset. She once famously declared, "I know what makes chicks tick." Fellow designer Vera Wang expanded on that thought when she said, "She [Stella] has a very special appreciation for women . . . It comes through in what she does. Let's face it, no man can ever know what it's really like to put on a bikini. And no man can know what a dress really feels like on your body."

Stella's Design Philosophy

"I think my design philosophy is to make clothes that allow women to reflect their inner confidence," Stella explained in an article in the *New Yorker*. She went on to say that her clothes "help women

Stella's own store, featuring her designs, was opened in London in 2003. McCartney now has retail stores in New York and Los Angeles, as well as a signature perfume, Stella.

have the confidence to be different and to be noticed, but in a very subtle, attractive kind of way. And it's a huge compliment when people fall for it."

For her part, Stella does not see herself in such grand terms. In an interview in the *Observer*, she briefly complained that her time is "cut up into little pieces," but then she caught herself and said, "It's OK, got a job. Better than nothing. I'm lucky I'm working."

Stella poses with Tom Ford, the designer for Gucci, at the 2002 launch party for *The Fashion* magazine.

Meanwhile, her business empire continues to expand. She now has shops in all the major fashion capitals of the world. And while her sales at the end of 2003 were perhaps not what her corporate bosses would have liked, few people doubt that, in time, profits will follow in the wake of her broad appeal. Tom Ford, who was until recently creative director at Gucci and, in effect, Stella's boss, told *New York* magazine, "She has everything it takes to be successful—the drive, the will, and the intelligence. She has great style, great taste. And she worries about the sales."

It's certain that Stella's brilliant fashion career will continue. Though, in the event it doesn't, she has a backup plan: "I must confess to being a frustrated musician," *ContactMusic*, a Web site, quoted her as saying. "For me, singing is the most natural thing in the world. I've grown up with it and I know that I've got that gift . . . I like to think that if people stop liking my clothes, I'll make a record."

Moving Forward After Loss

The years following Linda McCartney's death were difficult ones for the whole family. Paul frequently found himself overcome with emotion. "For about a year, I found myself crying—in all situations," he said in an interview with *Rolling Stone* magazine. "Anyone I met, anyone who came over, the minute we talked about Linda, I'd say, 'I'm sorry about this, I've got to cry.'" To help deal with such a great loss, Paul decided to throw himself into his work. He put the final touches on Linda's solo album, which was incomplete at the time of her death. He also recorded the album *Run Devil Run*, a collection of cover versions by such early influences as Little Richard, Fats Domino, Chuck Berry, and Elvis Presley.

PAUL McCARTNEY AND THE SEPTEMBER 11 ATTACKS

On September 11, 2001, Paul was taxiing on a New York airport runway when tragedy struck. On that day, terrorists flew airplanes into the World Trade Center's twin towers and the Pentagon. The McCartney plane never left the ground, and after returning to his home on Long Island, Paul decided to try to visit the scene of the disaster. He took a taxi and then walked around downtown Manhattan. "We just stood there, said a little prayer, and that was it," he explained in *Rolling Stone* magazine.

Paul was touched that the rescue workers recognized him. And he was determined to do something to help the city get back on its feet. He helped coordinate the Concert for New York City, organizing a musical lineup that included Mick Jagger, Keith Richards, David Bowie, Elton John, Melissa Etheridge, Eric Clapton, Billy Joel, and the Who. The concert raised more than $30 million for relief efforts and 9/11 victims' families. In an interview with *People* magazine a year later, Paul said that people still stop him on the street to say, "Hey, Paul, thanks for what you did for the city." His response, he told the magazine, is always the same: "It's my privilege."

A New Love

At about the same time he was working on *Run Devil Run*, Paul began dating Heather Mills, a former model who had become a full-time activist devoted to ridding the world of land mines. In June 2002, Sir Paul and Heather were married in a castle in the Irish town of Glaslough. The media made much of the fact that Heather's dress was not designed by Stella. Gossip about tensions between Stella and her stepmother has been a frequent subject in the tabloid press since Paul and Heather began dating. Wisely, Stella refuses to comment on her personal affairs.

Wedding Bells for Stella

In August 2003, Stella married her fiancé, magazine publisher Alasdhair Willis, on the tiny Scottish island of Bute. The ceremony was kept very private, but some facts have come out. Gwyneth Paltrow was the bridesmaid and guests included Madonna, actress Liv Tyler, Kate Moss, and Chrissie Hynde, singer and guitarist for the Pretenders and another famous vegetarian. As they were at Paul's wedding, guests were treated to vegetarian delights such as wild-mushroom pie and vegetarian sausages. Of course, Sir Paul was in attendance, along with Heather, who was seven months pregnant at the time. Mike McCartney, Paul's brother and Stella's uncle, told

In this 2002 photo, Paul and his future wife, Heather, are seen strolling the grounds of Castle Leslie in Ireland. Later that year, they held their wedding ceremony on the castle grounds.

Supermodel Kate Moss and lead singer for the Pretenders, Chrissie Hynde, arrive at the wedding of Stella McCartney and Alasdhair Willis. The ceremony took place in a secluded chapel at Mount Stuart, a gothic mansion on the picturesque island of Bute.

People magazine it was "lovely" and said all the couple wanted was "a quiet, peaceful wedding." Fortunately, this is what they got, thanks in no small part to the forty-man security force Paul hired for the occasion.

Meanwhile, Paul McCartney still tours as a rock performer, and he continues to expand his talents into a wide variety of other media, including classical music, painting, and animation.

In October 2003, Paul became a father at the age of sixty-one, when Beatrice Milly McCartney was born in London. His latest creative project is a perfect complement to his new embrace of fatherhood. The project— a DVD of children's animation—was done in collaboration with filmmaker Geoff Dunbar and longtime Beatles producer George Martin. Paul does all the music and voices for three short animations featuring frogs, squirrels, and wizards. In a recent online chat with the MSN Web network, Paul describes his life today: "I love it all, and every aspect of what I do involves its own challenges and the fact that there's quite a big variety of work between recording, animation, touring live, painting, etc. It keeps it fresh so I don't have a favorite pursuit, I love them all equally."

In this 2004 photograph, Stella and her husband, Alasdhair Willis, are leaving a party held at Stella's store. The party was thrown to celebrate the one-year anniversary of the store's opening.

TIMELINE

1942	• James Paul McCartney is born in Liverpool, England.
1945	• Second World War ends.
1956	• Paul's mother, Mary, dies of cancer.
1957	• John Lennon asks Paul McCartney to join his band, the Quarrymen.
1964	• The Beatles' appearance on *The Ed Sullivan Show* is watched by 70 million viewers.
1966	• The Beatles play their final concert in San Francisco.
1967	• *Sgt. Pepper's Lonely Hearts Club Band* is released.
1969	• Paul becomes engaged to Linda Eastman.
1970	• The Beatles disband. • Paul releases his first solo record, *McCartney*.
1971	• Stella McCartney is born. • Paul forms a new band, Wings.
1990	• Paul is awarded a lifetime achievement Grammy.
1991	• Paul releases his first classical effort, "Liverpool Oratorio."
1997	• Paul is knighted by Queen Elizabeth II. • Stella succeeds Karl Lagerfeld as chief fashion designer at Chloé.
1998	• Linda McCartney dies of breast cancer at age fifty-six.
1999	• Paul is inducted into the Rock and Roll Hall of Fame as a solo act. • Paul is named Greatest Composer of the Last 1,000 Years in a BBC poll.
2000	• Stella is named VH1/*Vogue* Designer of the Year.
2001	• Stella leaves Chloé to start her own company, which is backed by the Gucci Group. • Terrorists fly planes into the World Trade Center and the Pentagon. • Paul helps organize the Concert for New York City.
2002	• Paul marries Heather Mills.
2003	• Stella marries Alasdhair Willis. • Beatrice Milly McCartney is born to Paul and Heather McCartney.
2004	• *Paul McCartney: The Music and Animation Collection* is released by Miramax.

Beatlemania A word coined to describe the worldwide impact of the Beatles' popularity. Everywhere they went, John, Paul, George, and Ringo were met by worshipful fans, hysterical adulation, and denunciations by culture commentators.

Berry, Chuck Rock 'n' roll pioneer. Along with the Everly Brothers, Buddy Holly, Carl Perkins, Elvis Presley, and Little Richard, he was a major influence on the Beatles's music.

Chanel, Coco A famous French fashion designer.

couture One-of-a-kind custom-made pieces of clothing, usually meant to be shown at a fashion show.

faux Fake.

induct To admit as a member.

knighthood A title given by the queen of England as a way to honor a citizen of the United Kingdom for achievement or service to the country.

midwife A person trained to assist women in childbirth.

pop music A type of music characterized by simple melodies and catchy choruses.

rock 'n' roll A form of popular music usually featuring vocals, electric guitars, and a strong beat.

Saville Row A street in London that used to be famous for its custom men's tailors.

sitar A stringed instrument from India.

skiffle An informal "good time music" influenced by country, folk, and blues and played on washboard, tea-chest bass, Spanish guitar, and snare drum. Skiffle was a big influence on the Beatles when they were first playing.

Web Sites

Due to the changing nature of Internet links, the Rosen Publishing Group, Inc., has developed an online list of Web sites related to the subject of this book. This site is updated regularly. Please use this link to access the list:

http://www.rosenlinks.com/fafa/pmsm

FOR FURTHER READING

Barrow, Tony, and Robin Bexter. *Paul McCartney: Now and Then.* Milwaukee, Wisconsin: Hal Leonard, 2004.

Graham, Jorie. *Paul McCartney: I Saw Him Standing There.* New York: Watson-Guptill Publications, 2001.

Harry, Bill. *The Paul McCartney Encyclopedia.* London: Virgin Books, 2003.

McCartney, Paul, Caroline Grimshaw, and Bill Bernstein. *Each One Believing: On Stage, Off Stage, and Backstage.* San Francisco: Chronicle Books, 2004.

McGee, Garry. *Band on the Run: A History of Paul McCartney and Wings.* Lanham, Maryland: Taylor Trade Publishing, 2003.

Miles, Barry. *Paul McCartney: Many Years from Now.* New York: Henry Holt & Co., 1996.

Peel, Ian. *The Unknown Paul McCartney: McCartney and the Avant-Garde.* Richmond, Surrey (UK): Reynolds & Hearn, 2002.

BIBLIOGRAPHY

Armstrong, Lisa. "Stella Nova." *New York* magazine, August 25, 2002, reprinted on New York Metro Web site. Retrieved January 14, 2004 (http://www.newyorkmetro.com/shopping/articles/02/fallfashion/stellanova/index.htm).

Guinness Book of World Records. "Biggest All-Time Sales for a Band." The Guinness Web site. Retrieved May 22, 2004 (http://www.guinnessworldrecords.com/index.asp?id = 50910).

Owen, David. "Going Solo." *New Yorker*, September 17, 2001, pp. 130–139.

"Paul McCartney." *Newsmakers*, Issue 4. Gale Group, 2002. Reproduced in Biography Resource Center. Farmington Hills, MI: The Gale Group, 2004.

Spitz, Bob. "He May Be Sir Paul, but He's Still a Beatle." *New York Times*, May 25, 1997, section B, p. 26.

"Stella McCartney." *Contemporary Fashion*, 2nd ed. St. James Press, 2002. Reproduced in Biography Resource Center. Farmington Hills, MI: The Gale Group, 2004.

"Stella McCartney." *Newsmakers*, Issue 3. Gale Group, 2001. Reproduced in Biography Resource Center. Farmington Hills, MI: The Gale Group, 2004.

Synnot, Sibhan. "From Riches to Rags." *Scotland on Sunday*, December 14, 2003. Retrieved from Scotland on Sunday Web site January 12, 2004 (http://www.news.scotsman.com/opinion.cfm?id = 1371832003).

Wood, Gaby. "Hey Stella, Let's Do Launch." *The Observer*, May 18, 2003. Retrieved from the Guardian Web site January 22, 2004 (http://observer.guardian.co.uk/review/story/0,6903,958126,00.html).

INDEX

About the Author

Tim Ungs has a B.A. from the University of Notre Dame and an M.A. in English literature from the University of Minnesota.

Photo Credits

Cover (left) © Karwai Tang/Alpha/Globe Photos, Inc.; cover (right), back cover, pp. 1 (right), 13, 17, 18 (inset), 24 © AP World Wide Photos; p. 1 (left) © Nina Prommer/Globe Photos, Inc.; p. 1 (background) © Dave Benett/Getty Images; pp. 4, 21, 32 © Reuters/Corbis; p. 6 © Evan Agostin/Getty Images; p. 8 © Photo B. D. V./Corbis; p. 10 © Hulton-Deutsch Collection/Corbis; p. 15 © Ellis Robert/Corbis; p. 18 © Richard Melloul/Corbis; p. 22 © Orban Thierry/Corbis; p. 26 © Dejean/Nogues/Corbis; p. 28 © Goldberg Diego/Corbis; p. 31 © Jim Sugar/Corbis; p. 32 (inset) © Petre Buzoianu/Avantis/Time Life Pictures/Getty Images; p. 35 © Andrea Renault/Globe Photos, Inc.; p. 36 © James Peltekian/Corbis; p. 38 © Joe Dunne/Getty Images; p. 40 © Thompsett/Callega/Globe Photos, Inc.; p. 41 © Henry Davenport/Globe Photos, Inc.

Designer: Nelson Sá; **Editor:** Annie Sommers; **Photo Researcher:** Nelson Sá

Irvington Public Library
Irvington-on-Hudson, N.Y.
WITHDRAWN